D0468571

# BABY RECORD

## THE FIRST FIVE YEARS

IMAGES BY

# ANNE GEDDES

ANNE GEDDES ™

ISBN 0-8362-6599-8

© Anne Geddes 1997

Anne Geddes is the registered trademark of The Especially Kids Company Limited
Published in 1997 by Photogenique Publishers (a division of Hodder Moa Beckett)
Studio 3.16, Axis Building, 1 Cleveland Road, Parnell
Auckland, New Zealand

First Canadian edition published in 1997 by Andrews McMeel Publishing,
4520 Main Street, Kansas City, MO 64111-7701, USA

Designed by Frances Young
Produced by Kel Geddes
Color separations by MH Group

Printed through Midas Printing Limited, Hong Kong

All rights reserved. No part of this publication may be reproduced (except brief
passages for the purpose of a review), stored in a retrieval system or transmitted
in any form by any means, electronic, mechanical, photocopying, recording or otherwise,
without the proper written permission of the publisher.

*A*nne Geddes is an Australian born professional photographer living in Auckland, New Zealand.

*The worldwide success of her best selling book* Down in the Garden *continues to reinforce the title that Anne has earned of being the pre-eminent photographer of children in the world today.*

*Anne has said the following about her work, "I am frequently asked why I photograph babies so often, and where my ideas come from. Little babies are indeed my inspiration, and I cannot imagine a photographic life without them playing a major part in it. Where this special love for babies comes from I cannot tell you, and I have spent much time searching for an answer myself. All I know is that they are all perfect little human beings in their own ways, and we should all take the time to cherish them, especially while they are very small."*

*This book is intended to help you and your child cherish those unique, first five years in which so many changes and priceless moments occur.*

# Contents

# My Birth

# My Name is

I was born on _____

at _____

_____

The time was _____

I was delivered by _____

_____

I weighed _____

and measured _____

My eyes were _____

My hair color was _____

# Mementos

My Birth Announcement

A lock of hair

My hospital tag

# Newspaper Clippings

*What was happening in the world*

# Photographs

# Comments

*Mother* _____

_____

_____

_____

*Father* _____

_____

_____

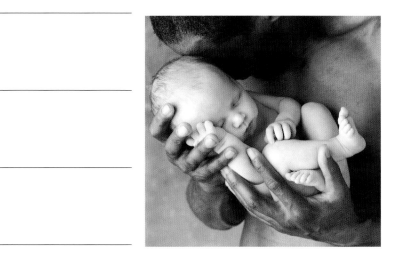

_____

# Special Messages

*Family* _____

_____

_____

_____

_____

*Friends* _____

_____

_____

_____

# Visitors and Gifts

# Signs

Star Sign _____

_____

Chinese Year _____

_____

Birth Stone _____

_____

Birth Flower _____

_____

# Naming

My full name is _____

My name was chosen by _____

because _____

My pet names are _____

Ceremonies celebrating my birth _____

at _____

Comments _____

_____

_____

# Photographs

# *My Family Tree*

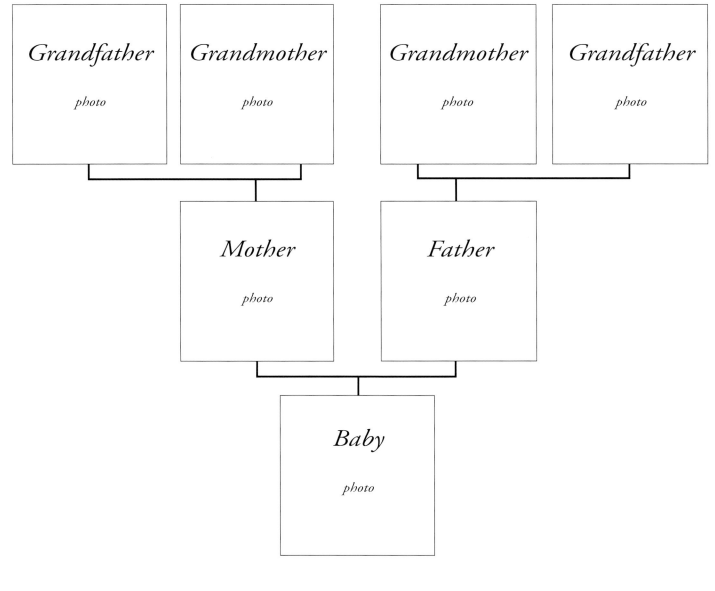

Grandfather — photo

Grandmother — photo

Grandmother — photo

Grandfather — photo

Mother — photo

Father — photo

Baby — photo

*I look like* _____

_____

# Photographs

*Brothers and Sisters*

# Three Months

*Weight* _____

*Length* _____

*Comments* _____

_____

_____

_____

_____

_____

# Photographs

# Six Months

*Weight* _____

*Length* _____

*Comments* _____

_____

_____

_____

_____

_____

# Photographs

# Nine Months

Weight _____

Length _____

Comments _____

_____

_____

_____

_____

_____

_____

# Photographs

# Milestones

I first smiled _____

laughed _____

grasped a toy _____

I held my head up _____

I slept through the night _____

rolled over _____

sat up _____

Comments _____

_____

*I first crawled* _____

*stood up* _____

*walked* _____

*My first tooth* _____

*My first word* _____

*Comments* _____

_____

_____

_____

# Food

My first solid food _____

I was weaned _____

I drank from a cup _____

Finger food _____

I fed myself _____

_____

*I like* _____

_____

_____

_____

_____

*I don't like* _____

_____

_____

_____

# My First Christmas

was at _____

Other people there _____

_____

_____

_____

My presents _____

_____

_____

_____

# Photographs

# My First Vacation

was at _____

Date _____

The weather was _____

Other people there _____

_____

Comments _____

_____

_____

# Photographs

# My First Birthday

I live at _____

My height is _____ Weight _____

My presents _____

_____

_____

_____

_____

_____

# *My Party*

Date _____

Where held _____

Friends and relations there _____

_____

_____

_____

_____

_____

_____

# Photographs

# Clothes

The first time I dressed myself _____

_____

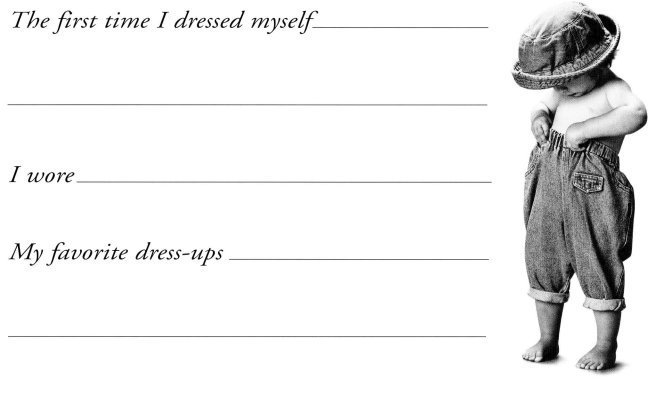

I wore _____

My favorite dress-ups _____

_____

I won't wear _____

_____

Comments _____

_____

# Photographs

# Favorites

Music _____

_____

_____

_____

Rhymes _____

_____

Clothes _____

_____

Animals _____

_____

*Activities* _____

_____

_____

*Television Programs* _____

_____

*I really don't like* _____

_____

_____

_____

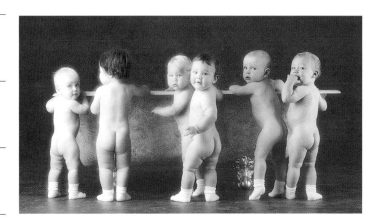

# Best Friends

One Year

*photo*

Two Years

*photo*

*Comments* _____

_____

Three Years

*photo*

_____

_____

## Four Years

*photo*

## Five Years

*photo*

## Comments ———————————————

———————————————————————————

———————————————————————————

———————————————————————————

———————————————————————————

# My Second Birthday

I live at _____

My height is _____ Weight _____

My presents _____

_____

_____

_____

_____

_____

_____

# My Party

Date _____

Where held _____

Friends and relations there _____

_____

_____

_____

_____

_____

_____

_____

# Photographs

# *My Third Birthday*

I live at _____

My height is _____ Weight _____

My presents _____

_____

_____

_____

_____

_____

_____

# My Party

Date _____

Where held _____

Friends and relations there _____

_____

_____

_____

_____

_____

_____

_____

# Photographs

# My Fourth Birthday

I live at _____

My height is _____ Weight _____

My presents _____

_____

_____

_____

_____

_____

# My Party

Date _____

Where held _____

Friends and relations there _____

_____

_____

_____

_____

_____

_____

# Preschool

I started on _____

at _____

My friends are _____

_____

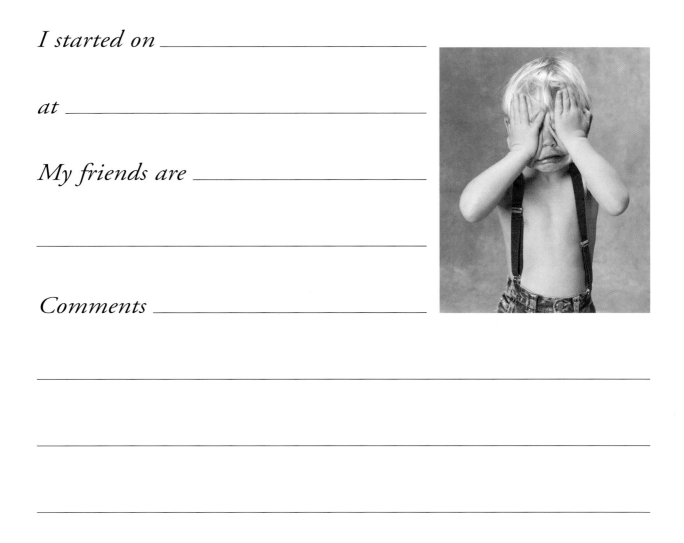

Comments _____

_____

_____

_____

_____

# Photographs

# Photographs

# My Fifth Birthday

I live at _____

My height is _____ Weight _____

My presents _____

_____

_____

_____

_____

_____

_____

# My Party

Date _____

Where held _____

Friends and relations there _____

_____

_____

_____

_____

_____

_____

# Photographs

# Kindergarten

My first day of kindergarten was on _____

at _____

My teacher is _____

Comments _____

_____

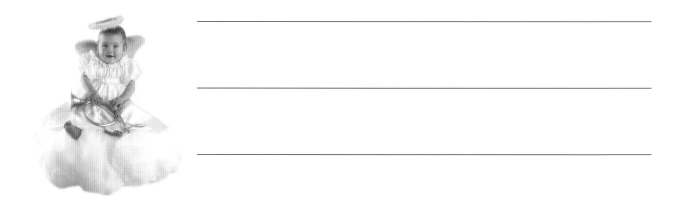

_____

_____

_____

_____

_____

# Photographs

# Drawings

# Writing

I could recite the alphabet _____

_____

I started to write _____

I began to read _____

My writing _____

_____

_____

_____

_____

# Health

Immunization

| Age | Vaccine | Date given |
|-----|---------|------------|
| | _____ | _____ |
| | _____ | _____ |
| _____ | _____ | _____ |
| | _____ | _____ |
| | _____ | _____ |
| _____ | _____ | _____ |
| | _____ | _____ |
| | _____ | _____ |
| _____ | _____ | _____ |
| | _____ | _____ |
| | _____ | _____ |
| _____ | _____ | _____ |
| | _____ | _____ |
| _____ | _____ | _____ |

*Allergies*_____

_____

_____

*Illnesses* _____

_____

_____

*Comments* _____

_____

_____

# My Height

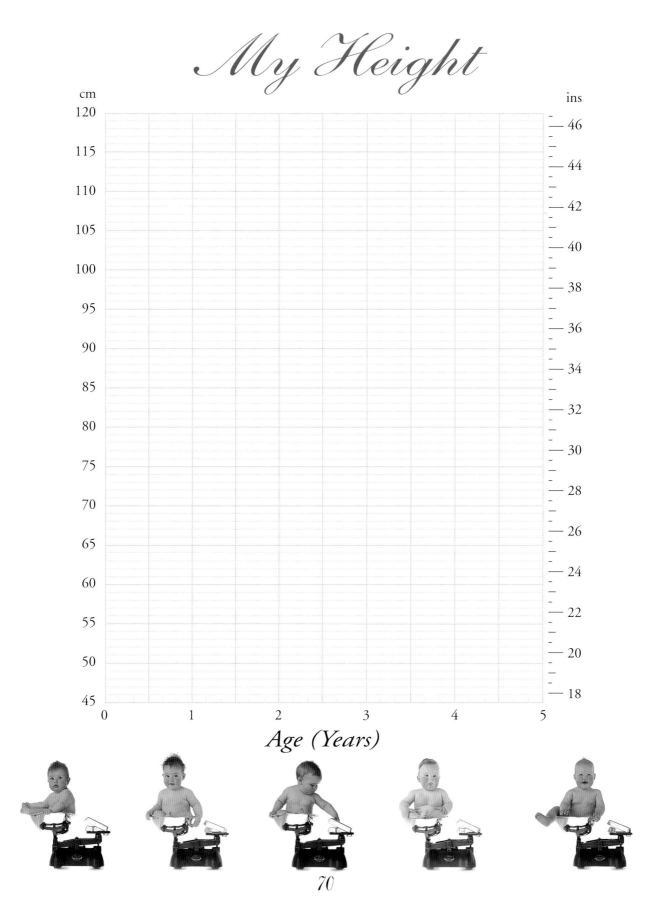

cm | ins

120 — 46
115 — 44
110 — 42
105 — 40
100 — 38
95 — 36
90 — 34
85 — 32
80 — 30
75 — 28
70 — 26
65 — 24
60 — 22
55 — 20
50 — 18
45

Age (Years)

0    1    2    3    4    5

# *My Weight*

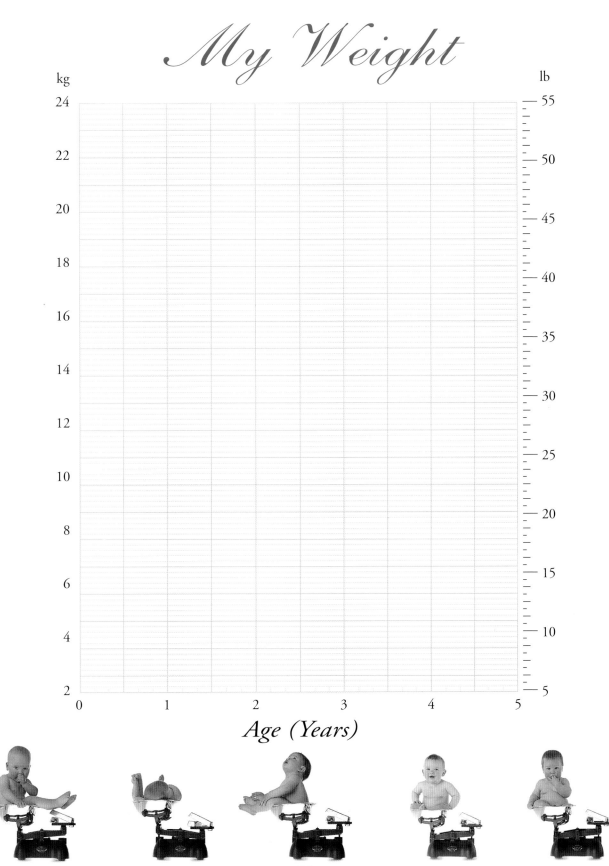

kg

lb

24 — 55

22 — 50

20 — 45

18 — 40

16 — 35

14 — 30

12 — 25

10 — 20

8

6 — 15

4 — 10

2 — 5

0        1        2        3        4        5

*Age (Years)*

# My Teeth

## Upper Jaw

Date

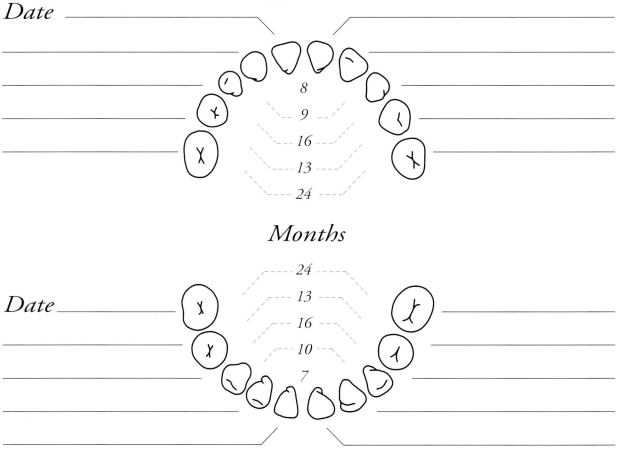

8
9
16
13
24

## Months

24
13
16
10
7

Date

## Lower Jaw

Visits to the dentist

# The Tooth Fairy's Page

I lost my first tooth on _____

My second tooth _____

The Tooth Fairy left me _____

_____

_____

Comments _____

_____

_____

_____

# My Handprints

At birth

At five years

# My Footprints

*At birth*

*At five years*

# Star Signs

## Capricorn

22 December – 20 January
Resourceful, self-sufficient, responsible

## Aquarius

21 January – 18 February
Great caring for others, very emotional
under cool exterior

## Pisces

19 February – 19 March
Imaginative, sympathetic, tolerant

## Aries

20 March – 20 April
Brave, courageous, energetic, loyal

## Taurus

21 April – 21 May
Sensible, love peace and stability

## Gemini

22 May – 21 June
Unpredictable, lively, charming, witty

## Cancer

22 June – 22 July
Love security, comfort

## Leo

23 July – 23 August
Idealistic, romantic, honorable, loyal

## Virgo

24 August – 23 September
Shy, sensitive, value knowledge

## Libra

24 September – 23 October
Diplomat, full of charm and style

## Scorpio

24 October – 22 November
Compassionate, proud, determined

## Sagittarius

23 November – 21 December
Bold, impulsive, seek adventure

# Birthstones

|  |  |
|---|---|
| January | Garnet – Constancy and truth |
| February | Amethyst – Sincerity, humility |
| March | Aquamarine – Courage and energy |
| April | Diamond – Innocence, success |
| May | Emerald – Tranquillity |
| June | Pearl – Precious, pristine |
| July | Ruby – Freedom from care, chastity |
| August | Moonstone – Joy |
| September | Sapphire – Hope, chastity |
| October | Opal – Reflects every mood |
| November | Topaz – Fidelity, loyalty |
| December | Turquoise – Love and success |

# Flowers

|  |  |
|---|---|
| January | Snowdrop – Pure and gentle |
| February | Carnation – Bold and brave |
| March | Violet – Modest |
| April | Lily – Virtuous |
| May | Hawthorn – Bright and hopeful |
| June | Rose – Beautiful |
| July | Daisy – Wide-eyed and innocent |
| August | Poppy – Peaceful |
| September | Morning Glory – Easily contented |
| October | Cosmos – Ambitious |
| November | Chrysanthemum – Sassy and cheerful |
| December | Holly – Full of foresight |

*Comments* _____

_____

_____

_____

_____

_____

_____

_____

# Photographs

*Comments*

# Photographs